My
FiRST
BOOK OF
Nature

Seashore

Victoria Munson

WAYLAND

First published in 2017 by Wayland
Copyright © Hodder and Stoughton 2017

Wayland
Carmelite House
50 Victoria Embankment
London
EC4Y 0DZ

Editor: Victoria Brooker
Designer: Elaine Wilkinson

A cataloguing record for this title is
available at the British Library.

ISBN: 978 1 5263 0153 6

Printed in China

Wayland, part of Hachette Children's
Group and published by Hodder
and Stoughton Limited.
www.hachette.co.uk

Acknowledgements:
Istock: 5b zoerae28; 6 milynmiles; 21t Rex_
Wholster; Shutterstock: cover main David
Osborn; (bl) Nicolas Primola; (tl) Raymond
Llewellyn; (br) Bjoern Buxbaum Conradi;
(tr) Peter Moulton; (mr) Tamara Kulikova;
2t, 17 Joao Pedro Silva; 2b, 11 lobster20;
3t, 13 Emi; 3b Lorna Munden; 4 Triple H
Images; 5t DJTTaylor; 7t Aleksey Stemmer;
8Paul Nash; 9t Ruud Morijn Photographer;
9b Johnson76; 10 Zharate; 11t Martin
Fowler; 11b lobster20; 12 Arto Hakola;
13t Florian Andronache; 13b V. Belov; 14
Randimal; 14b Steve McWilliam; 15t Ger
Bosma Photos; 15b Jausa; 16 MP cz; 17t
Seaphotoart; 17b Joao Pedro Silva; 18t Tory
Kalliman; 18b Willyam Bradberry; 19t David
Osborn; 19b Andrew M. Allport; 20 Becky
Stares; 21b C Tatiana; Naturepl 7b Sue Daly;

MIX
Paper from
responsible sources
FSC® C104740
FSC
www.fsc.org

Contents

What is the Seashore?

The seashore is the point where land meets sea. Seashores can be sandy, rocky or pebbly.

Seashores are home to many different plants and animals.

Twice a day, the sea moves up the shore and back down again. These movements are called tides. At high tide, waves are at the top part of the beach. Low tide is when the sea is at the lowest part of the beach.

Some beaches have rock pools.
Fish hide when a shadow
covers their rock pool.

Animals such
as anemones
and crabs live
in rock pools.

Many sea animals stay in the same
place so it is easy to spot them.

Tide
times are
different
every day.
Check the tide
times before you set
out to the seashore.

The best time to look for
nature on the beach is
when the tide is out.

5

Rock pool creatures

Acorn barnacles have grey-white shells with a diamond-shaped opening at the top. When the tide is out, the shell will be closed.

When under water, the acorn barnacles open and stick out feathery limbs.

Acorn barnacles are the most common type of barnacle in the UK.

Shore crabs are a brownish-green colour. All crabs have four pairs of legs and a front pair of pincers. Pincers are used to fight and catch prey.

Female crabs can lay up to **185,000** eggs at a time.

Shore crabs eat barnacles and dog whelks.

Shanny fish are green-brown with dark blotches that look like pebbles. This makes them hard to spot in rock pools.

Look for shanny fish hiding under stones.

Shanny fish are also called blennies.

Seaweed

Egg wrack sticks to rocks using a 'holdfast', which is a round, root-like growth.

Egg wrack air bladders are egg-shaped.

You can estimate the age of egg wrack by counting the bladders as one bladder grows each year.

Bladderwrack gets its name from its rounded air bladders.

These air bladders help the seaweed to **float** in the sea.

Bladderwrack is used for food and medicine.

Sea lettuce clings to rocks using a holdfast. It looks crumpled and reminds people of lettuce leaves.

Sea lettuce can be cooked and eaten and is full of vitamins and minerals.

Shells

Shells are homes for soft-bodied creatures called molluscs.

Limpets have grey-white cone-shaped shells.

When the tide is in, they move around on rocks. As the tide goes out, they return to the same spot by following the mucus trail they left behind.

There is sometimes a dent in the rock where limpets have been because they return to the same spot so often.

Dog whelks usually have creamy-yellowish or light grey shells. They can also be orange, yellow, brown or black.

Dog whelks were used in Anglo-Saxon times to produce purple dyes.

Dog whelks make holes in limpet shells and suck out the flesh inside.

Cockle shells have a creamy brown, ridged shell.

Cockles are eaten by humans, fish and birds.

Birds

Black-headed gulls get their name from their black head. However, it is only black in summer.

For the rest of the year, black-headed gulls have a white head with chocolate-brown stripes.

Herring gulls have a hooked yellow bill with a red spot.

Herring gulls are **large,**

NOISY BIRDS.

In winter, their head is streaked with grey-brown marks. For the rest of the year their head is white.

Oystercatchers have black and white bodies with a long, bright orange beak.

Oystercatchers will sometimes use gull's nest to lay their eggs in.

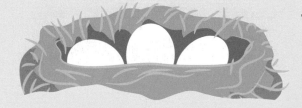

Oystercatchers use their long beak to break open limpet shells to eat them.

Insects

Cinnabar moths have bright red stripes and spots on a black body.

The red colour warns other insects not to eat them.

They are most active at night, but can sometimes be seen in the daytime too.

Cinnabar moth caterpillars are also brightly coloured, with thick black and gold stripes.

Common blue butterflies can be found on flowers near sand dunes.

The upper side of their wings is blue, but the underside is grey-brown with orange markings.

Sand digger wasps have a black body with a bright orange waist.

They sting caterpillars and then drag them back to their nest.

The wasps lay their eggs inside the caterpillars' bodies. When the wasp eggs hatch, the new-born larvae eat the caterpillars.

Fish

Rock gobies are covered in dark brown blotches that make them hard to spot.

Gobies lay up to **7,000 eggs** at one time.

Gobies have suckers on fins underneath their bodies. These suckers help them stick to rocks so that they aren't washed away.

Tompot blenny fish have big round eyes, a large head and a thin body.

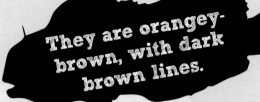

They are orangey-brown, with dark brown lines.

Tompot blennies have feathery tentacles on top of their head.

Two-spot gobies are small thin fish. They get their name from the two black spots on their body.

Two-spot gobies can be red, green, pinky-orange or brown.

Mammals

Bottlenose dolphins are grey with a long bottle-shaped beak.

Bottlenose dolphins like to follow boats and can be seen leaping out of the water beside them.

Dolphins have a blowhole on the top of their head through which they get air.

A group of dolphins is called a pod.

Grey seals are common along the west coast of Britain.

Grey seals are blue-grey and are often seen floating with just their head out of the water.

Grey seal pups have white fur when they are born.

Common seals are found along the east coast of the UK. They have a rounded face. Common seals are brown or grey with dark spots.

In water, common seals can reach speeds of 30 kph.

Plants

Marram grass is the tall and spiky grass that grows in and around sand dunes.

Its glossy thin leaves are rolled up to hold in water.

Marram grass has long roots to help it find water. The roots also hold the sand in sand dunes together to stop them being blown away.

Yellow-horned poppies have bright yellow petals. The leaves are thick and rough.

Sap from yellow-horned poppy's stems is very poisonous.

Yellow-horned poppies get their name from the seed pods, which are long and curved like elephants' tusks.

Thrift has round, pink, flower heads. It has tall hairy stems. Thrift leaves are tightly packed together forming a cushion on the ground.

Thrift is also known as sea pink, ladies' cushion and Mary's pillow.

Seashore Shells

At the seashore, see what empty shells you can find.

1

Periwinkles
Periwinkles have a thick, rounded shell with grey-brown spirals. Sometimes they have a sharp point on the end, although the point eventually gets worn away by the sea.

2

Limpets
Limpets are grey-white cone-shaped shells. Limpets higher up the shore will have taller shells than those found on the lower shore.

Mussels

Mussels are often found together in large numbers on rocks. The shells are long bluish-purplish ovals. The inside of the shell is smooth and pearly.

3

Laver spires

Laver spires are long, spiral-shaped, yellow-brown shells.

4

Dog Whelks

Dog whelk shells are usually creamy-yellowish or light grey, but they can also be shades of orange, yellow, brown or black.

5

Cockles

Cockle shells are creamy-white and brown with ridges.

6

Glossary and Index

larvae the young worm-like stage in an insect's life cycle

suckers part of an animal's body used for attaching to things

tentacles flexible arms of an animal used for grabbing things and moving